IMAGES OF
Loughborough

IMAGES OF
Loughborough

LEICESTERSHIRE
COUNTY COUNCIL
LIBRARIES AND
INFORMATION SERVICE

Breedon Books
Publishing Company
Derby

First published in Great Britain by
The Breedon Books Publishing Company Limited
Breedon House, 44 Friar Gate, Derby, DE1 1DA.
1999

ISBN 1 85983 161 3

Printed and bound by Butler & Tanner Ltd., Selwood Printing Works,
Caxton Road, Frome, Somerset.

Colour separations by GreenShires Ltd, Leicester.

Jackets printed by Lawrence-Allen, Avon.

Contents

Introduction

THE purpose of this book is to release a sample of the 4,000 photographs in Loughborough Library's Local Studies Collection. This collection, unknown even to many natives of the town, is a valuable store of Loughborough's history. As well as photographs there are books, periodicals, newspapers, maps and family history sources. These are being added to constantly, with donations from the public especially welcome.

The Granby Street library has been part of the scene since 1905, providing both enlightenment and entertainment to generations of Loughborough people. Originally the old Corporation's town library, it became part of Leicestershire County Council's network of libraries in 1974. Since then it has expanded its services to include feature films on video, CD-Roms and Internet access.

The library's work in recording Loughborough's narrative is made all the more challenging by the fact that the town has such a long and fascinating history. Today, Loughborough no longer endures plagues, fires and Luddite riots as it once did, but it still maintains its market and November fair established by royal charter in the 1220s. The Victorian industrial heritage continues to dominate the Derby Road and Nottingham Road areas, while Loughborough University pursues the tradition of excellence in education established by the Grammar School and Loughborough College.

As the new Loughborough steps confidently into the 21st century, it may reflect with pride on past achievements and honour the memory of the men and women who made Loughborough the prosperous and vibrant place it is today.

About the Town

Loughborough Market Place *c.*1880s. A large crowd has gathered apparently awaiting the arrival of some important visitor. It is possible that it is the Royal Jubilee in 1887.

The Market Place in 1870. The inn sign to the right is that of the Plough Inn, which ended its days as an ironmongers' establishment. The man in the top hat is Joseph Giles, one of Loughborough's foremost solicitors. He died at the Cedars, Nanpantan, on 15 April 1893, aged 84.

Devonshire Square, photographed about 1895. The horse and cart driver and his friends take time out to pose for the camera.

The Market Place in the summer of 1900. On the right are the premises known in 1836 as the Ship Liquor Vaults and kept by Thomas Bryan. After he died, his widow took a Mr James into partnership. He eventually took complete control and after his death in 1900, his name lived on in the James's Vaults until Boots The Chemist built new premises on the site in 1958.

Well-to-do gentlemen in Loughborough Market Place towards the end of the 19th century.

The Market Place *c*.1904. The lady in the foreground is examining the produce.

Motorised transport now makes an appearance in this 1920s picture of Loughborough Market Place. Unlike today it seemed to be a case of 'park where you like'.

North side of the Market Place, pictured in 1927. Lipton's was opened on 26 March 1908, in premises formerly occupied by the Manchester Warehouse.

A view of the Market Place in the very early 1930s, showing the pavement marking the old building line, and the new buildings making the present frontage.

Another picture of the Market Place in the early 1930s. The ice cream seller waits patiently for a customer.

Children queue outside Potter's shop in the Market Place, waiting to buy fireworks, the first time they were available after the end of World War Two.

This picture was taken through the arch of the gateway to Keightley's shop in 1957 and shows the old Woolworth building which was demolished the following year to make way for a new Woolworth store.

A night-time view of Loughborough's November Fair, taken in the early 1950s.

Market Street in 1932, as crowds of onlookers watch mopping-up operations after a flood.

Two women take a stroll on a summer's day in Market Street in 1959, one of the hottest years on record. Further up the street, mothers push their babies in prams.

Derby Square and Swan Street in 1970. The scene is now much changed. The Green Man pub was replaced by a new pub of the same name a few dozen yards down the road, but eventually that too closed, to make way for a covered shopping centre.

Derby Square in July 1956, showing Gallagher & O'Brien's wallpaper and paint business. It is now a bridal-wear shop.

Swan Street in the 1920s before road widening.

The entrance to Swan Street from Derby Square, looking towards the Market. The Saracen's Head and the buildings beyond were demolished in 1931, the new Saracen's Head being built on the left-hand side of the old building.

Flooding at the junction of Ashby Road with Derby Road in the 1930s.

Derby Road in 1938, looking towards the town, and in the opposite direction. Both photographs were taken from near the end of Regent Street.

The group of property in Ashby Road known as Holborn Hill, pictured in the 1920s. The opening is that of William Street and the scaffolding marks the erection of the College buildings.

Ashby Road's corner with Frederick Street in 1969. The buildings on the corner were later demolished to make way for a large block of flats.

The Old Toll House at corner of Ashby and Cumberland Roads, which was removed about 1875. Pritchard's rope walk began immediately on the right of the photograph.

Hastings Street, Loughborough, pictured in 1973.

Looking from Fennel Street towards Lemington Street in 1963. The buildings on the right have since been demolished.

Ashby Square, pictured in the 1960s.

Church Gate, Loughborough, from Biggin Hill, photographed *c*.1900.

The entrance to Steeple Row, Church Gate. It was demolished in 1913 and made way for a new road and gardens at the side of the Church. Steeple Row (below) was perhaps the worst slum in Loughborough. The properties were owned by All Saints' Church.

Bedford Square, *c.*1954 looking from the Post Office towards Devonshire Square and the Market Place.

There is much activity at Loughborough Cattle Market in the 1880s.

A sale of plants on 25 May 1905, outside Armstrong's premises in the Cattle Market. These premises, together with those next door, ended their days as the grocery business of George Hill's County Stores. On the site later stood the Elmo supermarket.

The Cattle Market in the 1960s, showing Elmo's supermarket where once stood the County Stores and earlier still, Armstrong's.

The Cattle Market pictured one Monday in 1957, from Granby Street.

High Street looking from the Cross Keys Hotel towards Market, *c*.1900. On the extreme left is the piano shop of Herbert Marshall, who was Mayor of Leicester.

The Bull's Head Hotel sign straddles High Street towards the end of the 19th century.

A later view of High Street when horse-drawn wagons had been replaced by motor vehicles.

High Street in April 1929, as the front portion of the King's Head is demolished.

The corner of High Street and Baxter Gate in the 1920s.

The building jutting out on the pavement on the right of Baxter Gate was demolished in 1890 to make way for the Constitutional Club, which in turn was pulled down in the early 1930s to be replaced by the Conservative Club building.

Shops adjacent to the Hospital in Baxter Gate, removed for the extension to the Hospital in 1931.

Baxter Gate, *c.*1920s. The Corporation Electricity Showrooms are on the right side near the bottom of the street.

Baxter Gate from Marshall Green's shop looking towards High Street *c.*1928-29.

Baxter Gate before road widening. The pub on the left is the Rose and Crown, run by Frank Wilson.

Another view of Baxter Gate, this time further from the Rose and Crown which was demolished when the street was widened. A new licensed establishment was built in its place and called the Loughborough Hotel.

A court off Baxter Gate which was demolished in 1958.

Sparrow Hill, Loughborough, pictured in the 1890s.

Cottages at Meadow Lane, near its junction with Sparrow Hill. They were removed in 1928.

A fire insurance plaque on the wall of 21 Sparrow Hill.

Church Gate looking towards the Old Manor House on the corner of Sparrow Hill. The railings and gates on the right of the picture belong to the old Lancastrian School. The site of the building in the foreground became Lemington Street.

Church Gate in the late 1880s. The cart belonged to William B. Beckworth, aerated water manufacturer of Cademan Street, Whitwick. The sign over the pavement on the left denotes the premises of Claypoole & Sons, watchmakers, jewellers and pawnbrokers.

Another view of Church Gate, probably taken in the 1950s.

This photograph shows the lower end of Church Gate about 1896. On the left is Mr J. S. Hepworth's chemist's shop. In May 1913, Mr Hepworth was cycling across the Big Meadow when an aeroplane landed and the pilot asked him for directions to York.

The upper storey over Princes, Church Gate, pictured in January 1967.

Houses in Pinfold Street in 1957. They were demolished two years later.

A lady pauses with her small child in a pram outside the Three Horse Shoes on Nottingham Road, Loughborough, *c*.1890.

The Nottingham Road end of Conery Passage, showing the Royal George Inn which was pulled down in 1925 and rebuilt, set back to a new line. The wall under the trees was also rebuilt nearer the right-hand side of the photograph, making a wide entrance which became known as the Coneries. The term refers to the rabbit warrens used as a food source by the mediaeval manor house.

Nottingham Road pictured in 1960. The Methodist Church was demolished and a petrol station now stands on the site. Towle's factory – the large building on the right – has now closed down and its machinery has been removed. The Clarence Inn, on the far right of the picture, is now the Jack O'Lantern.

Mill Lane, off Nottingham Road, looking towards the old Clarence Inn. This picture was taken in 1971.

Repairs to the highway using a fine-looking steam roller in Leicester Road in the early part of the 20th century.

The junction of Southfield Road and Leicester Road in *c*.1881, showing the original gate to Southfields Park and site of the present lodge and entrance.

Looking down Woodgate towards the rebuilt corner of Packhorse Lane in December 1930. The old Baptist Chapel (now long since demolished) is on the right.

Woodgate, opposite the Baptist Chapel, *c.*1928.

Young girls pictured after Sunday School at the top of Toothill Road *c.*1900. On the left is the wall of the Rectory.

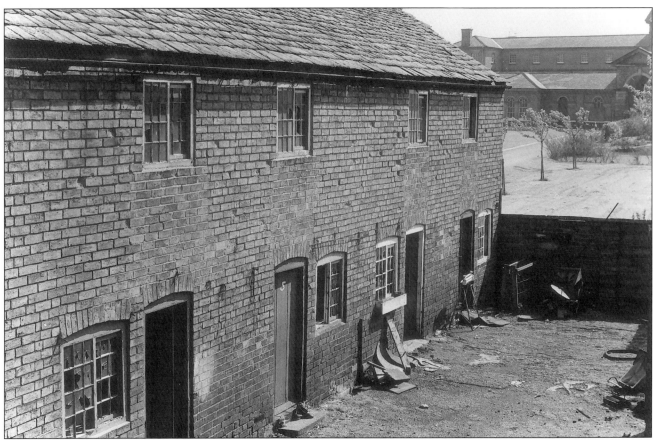

Rear of cottages in Union Lane, photographed in 1969.

Everyone poses for the camera in Burton Walks, *c.*1896.

Burton Walks in 1957. Despite protests from residents, many of the old elms were cut down because they were affected by Dutch Elm Disease and potentially dangerous because, whilst looking healthy, trees rot inside and can shed massive branches without warning. The lime trees which replaced the elms at Burton Walks are immune from the disease.

Public Buildings

Loughborough Town Hall pictured in October 1950. Next door, to the right, is the Old Boot Hotel and looking up the street is the 'Fifty Shilling Taylors'.

Fifteen years later, the scene hasn't changed a great deal. It must be market day because stalls are blocking the view through the Market Place.

What it could have looked like. The original proposed design for the Carillon Tower as a war memorial for Loughborough.

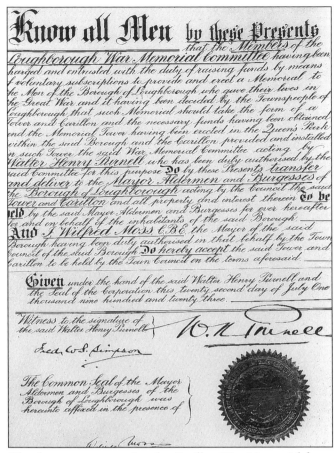

The document conveying the Carillon War Memorial from the Loughborough War Memorial Committee to the Loughborough Corporation on 22 July 1923.

The bells for Loughborough Carillon Tower were hoisted from the lorries bringing them from John Taylor's Works (see also *The Industrial Scene*) by means of a Morris pulley block. Afterwards they were lifted on to the Carillon frame at the top of the tower by hoisting them through holes in the centre of the various floors.

The bells in place in the Carillon.

The Carillon and Queen's Park, photographed from the top of the multi-storey car park in Granby Street in 1965. The car park was later demolished.

Island House in Granby Street with the Carillon in the background. This building was demolished in 1964 to make way for the terracotta-faced CLASP extension to the Public Library.

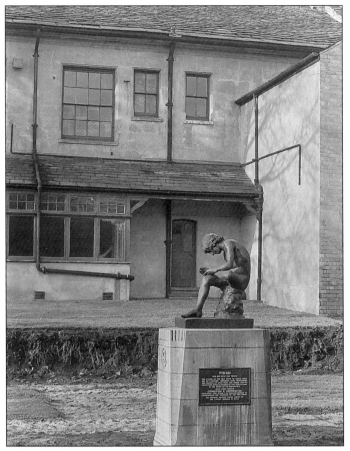

The former Island House, showing the statue of the boy with a thorn in his foot, a gift from Loughborough's twin town in France, Epinal.

The Public Library in Granby Street, probably photographed around the time of its completion in 1905.

Another view of the Public Library in Granby Street, this time pictured from further up the street and dated no later than 1964 because it has not been extended.

Mr T. D. Pearce, Borough Librarian from 1943 to 1960, seated centre, with members of his staff at the Public Library in Granby Street.

The old Public Library and Town Offices in Greenclose Lane, all now demolished. The posters advise youngsters to 'Aim high' and join the Loughborough College Junior School of Art. The men on the ladder are all wearing firemen's helmets, though not all are in uniform.

Staff of the old Post Office in Baxter Gate gather for a group photograph in 1897, to mark the diamond jubilee of Queen Victoria.

Nearly 60 years on and fashions had changed considerably by the late 1950s as shown by this group of Loughborough General Post Office staff posed for a cameraman outside the GPO building on the corner of the Coneries and Sparrow Hill.

The old bank premises at the corner of the High Street and Market Place. For many years they were occupied by the Nottingham and Nottinghamshire Banking Company until that bank's removal to the Cattle Market in June 1887. The building then became the Consumer's Tea Company premises.

The premises of the Leicestershire Banking Company, erected in 1893 and photographed here *c.*1900. Afterwards it became the London City and Midland Bank Ltd and then the home of the Midland Bank.

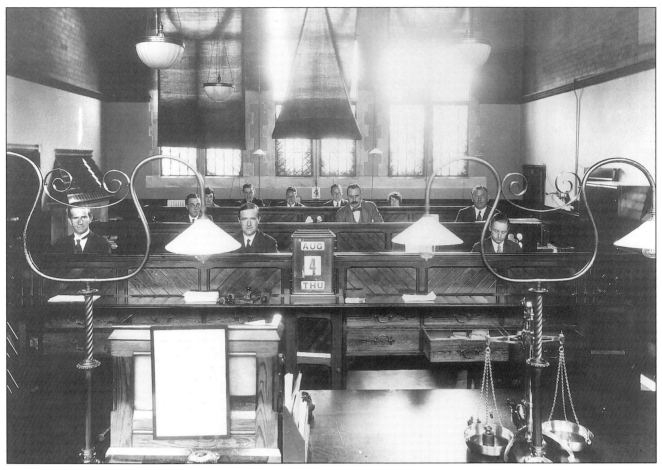

Two photographs of the interior and staff of the Westminster Bank on 4 August 1927.

The Board of Guardians outside the Workhouse on Derby Road, probably early in the 20th century.

The boardroom of the Workhouse on Derby Road.

The handsome tower of the Victory Cinema in Biggin Street, photographed in January 1967.

The audience is gathered for the opening of the Theatre Royal in Market Street in 1905.

Loughborough General Hospital, probably photographed *c*.1910 before alterations.

Shopping Around

The staff of Edwin Moss, grocer's, of High Street, posing outside the premises at the junction with Baxter Gate in the latter half of the 19th century.

Cornelius Wooding had premises at 16 Church Gate, where he sold national and local newspapers. He was, however, primarily a bill poster and placard writer and advertised that he could post bills 'in town or country by the week, month or year' in Loughborough, Leicester and surrounding villages. In 1877 he issued a statement that 'malicious parties' were trying 'to take the roof from his head' and that he had to 'live in a tent', which may explain the state of his premises shown in this photograph. Nevertheless, it was at 16 Church Gate that he died on 31 January 1889.

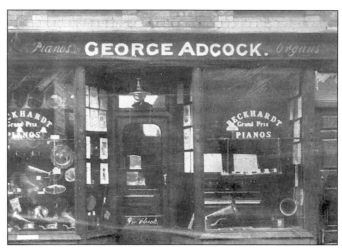

The Loughborough Pianoforte, American Organ and General Music Warehouse of George Adcock at 11 Baxter Gate, as it was *c.*1890. By then the business had been established for 45 years.

The jeweller's shop of Benjamin Baldwin at 7 Market Place, Loughborough. The son of a Nottingham outfitter, Baldwin came to Loughborough as an apprentice to Mr Gray and ultimately succeeded to the business. He is pictured here in the doorway of his premises. He died at his shop on 25 January 1893.

George Merrin stands in the doorway of his baker's business at 65-66 Sparrow Hill, *c.*1890s.

The auction mart of Garton & Amatt in Baxter Gate in 1897 and some 70 years later. The architecture of this rather curious building had been described as 'Scotch Baronial'. In the earlier picture, a poster on the window advertises building land in Toothill Road, and the Beacon Restaurant and Dining Rooms are to the right.

The house furnishing business premises of W. Caldwell & Son in Baxter Gate in 1910.

W. Caldwell & Son had moved to the Coneries by 1931 and seemed to have added Cadbury's chocolate to their range of goods.

Jonas Watkins, Frank W. Topping and Starkie T. Topping pictured outside the premises of Topping & Sons, who sold books and greetings cards, at the corner of Leicester Road and Woodgate. This photograph was taken *c.*1903.

A sight to make any vegetarian shudder. Bailey's butcher's shop at 2 Church Gate, Loughborough, around the turn of the century.

The Labour Bookshop in Market Street in 1919. There is an advertisement for a meeting of Shepshed Labour Party and the *Daily Herald* offers itself as 'The Paper for the Ex-Serviceman'.

The High Street butcher's shop of Herbert Martin, who took over soon after John Moss left it at the end of 1907. Pictured here in the early 1920s are Ted Hanford and Percy Rice.

J. T. Bolesworth's fish and game dealers in High Street. Next door to the left is Arthur C. Foxon's chiropodist's business. The picture was taken in the early 1920s.

The Market Street front of Simpkin & James's general provisions shop, showing the door to the right which gave access to the living accommodation above. This window display shows off wines and spirits but the shop also sold groceries and corn.

A more general view of the large premises of Simpkin & James in the Market Place. They were an upmarket grocery and provisions store.

These premises, formerly the Plough Inn, were acquired by Ison's as an ironmonger's establishment about 1870. Beeby & Henton, then T. Beeby, and finally T. & F. Keightley carried on the same trade there until the building was demolished in 1958.

Pickworth & Son's skin, hearth and rug merchants in Biggin Street in the 1920s. To the right, on the corner, is Hepworth's clothes shop which is offering a holiday wear sale, and to the left is the Red Lion public house.

Pickworth & Son's eventually took over Hepworth's site but then the whole lot was demolished. In this picture the top half of Hepworth's old building has already gone and Pickworth's are advertising, 'Pulling down shops. Goods sold at 40 per cent to 80 per cent off.'

The High Street draper's business of Young, Pilsbury & Young. These were the company's second premises and were demolished in 1928, along with the adjacent Old Bull's Head Hotel.

The replacement premises for Young, Pilsbury & Young, still in High Street, pictured in 1929. These later became Pilsbury & Towle.

Short & Bee, hosiers and hatters, occupied part of the Market Place building which in the late 1920s was demolished and rebuilt to the same plan in Baxter Gate. Mr Bee later had premises in High Street.

Three Market Place businesses pictured in 1929 – Martin's chemist's shop, Pearson's drapery establishment and Latimer's, also a chemist's. The terracotta front was by the Hathern Station Brick & Terracotta Co Ltd.

Paltridge's music shop in the lower end of Church Gate *c.*1930. It had been there since the late 1890s but was demolished in the 1960s. Alderman Bumpus had once had a clockmaker's and jeweller's shop here and when the building was pulled down traces of a large public clock could still be seen on the wall above the shop.

J. W. Barker's bakery business in Market Street in the 1930s. 'For reliable bread – everything home-made' was the company's proud boast.

The clothing shop of John S. Marr in Church Gate, photographed in the early 1930s. Third from left is Mr Mottershaw with Mr Leon Hall on his right.

This picture shows the saddlery business of Thompson's in the Bull's Head Yard which led to High Street. The taller building on the left is the Lord Nelson, Market Place, before rebuilding c.1935.

Clemerson's furnishing, carpet and linoleum store and removals firm in the Market Place, about the time the business closed down.

Another view of Clemerson's premises in 1971, after the company had closed. A popular Loughborough business, it had expanded over the years by taking over a miscellany of neighbouring premises.

The Industrial Scene

An old cotton-winding wheel in use with hand-frame stocking-making machines.

John Taylor made these jubilee bells for All Saints' Church in 1887.

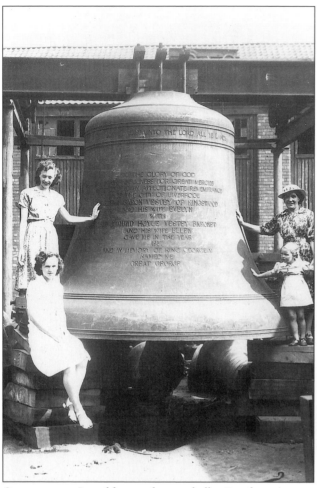

Some more Loughborough-cast bells. In the picture above the bells are dated 1937 and there is a reference to the city of Liverpool and to the late King George V. In the below picture, the date is 1908.

Casting the bells for Loughborough Carillon at John Taylor's in 1923.

Works and office staff of Messenger & Co of Loughborough, photographed in 1899. Works manager William Brooks (standing, bearded, third from right) joined the firm in 1866. He started his working career when he was only eight, and at 12 years old was apprenticed to Isaac Foster, a local blacksmith.

These women were employed at Messenger's during World War One to make munitions for the war effort.

Building the turbine shop at Brush Works. In 1893 it was announced that only 30 of the company's employees had moved with the firm from London instead of the 200 expected.

Brush Company Falcon works photographed from the Midland Goods Yard *c.*1896. Note the famous falcon which is now in the National Tramway Museum, Crich, Derbyshire.

A horse-drawn carriage negotiates floods at the Brush Works on 3 December 1910.

Aerial view of the Brush Works in the early 1960s.

Staff at Thomas Clarke & Son's dyeworks, Cattle Market, Loughborough, *c.*1890s.

Dyeworkers take a welcome rest as a photographer records life at Thomas Clarke's in the 1920s.

Lorries loaded at Thomas Clarke's dyeworks, Cattle Market, in the 1920s.

A driver about to take a big load from Thomas Clarke's in the Cattle Market.

A Herbert Morris lorry decorated for a carnival in 1934.

Morris Cranes factory from the Canal Bank in Allsopps Lane, pictured in 1971.

Charles Hulin, coachbuilder of High Street, pictured with an example of his work in September 1922.

The shop of Mr W. F. Charles in Baxter Gate, where he started his perfumery business which as Zenobia he sold to Genatosan in 1948. This photograph must have been taken before March 1888, by which date Mr Charles had transferred his premises to 38 Market Place. This Baxter Gate shop later housed the *Loughborough Monitor* newspaper.

Zenobia Perfumes employees of the 1920s.

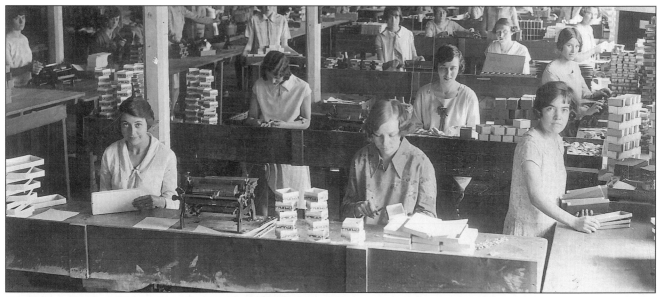

Workers at the Zenobia perfume factory in the late 1920s.

Members of Loughborough Rotary Club on a visit to Fort Dunlop on 29 April 1930. Standing centre right, in the light suit, is Captain Charles Huston, then managing director of Zenobia Perfumes.

Captain Charles Huston, managing director of Zenobia Perfumes, pictured at the company's stand at a trade exhibition in the 1930s. Captain Huston had married the daughter of Zenobia's founder, Mr W. F. Charles.

Highly-polished vehicle outside the Willowbrook Bus Works in 1934.

Employees of Loughborough Corporation Gas Department in 1928.

Production line at Towles Ltd in the 1930s.

T. P. Towles Ltd's spinning factory on Queen's Road in 1948. Formerly Cartwright and Warner's which had gone out of business in 1929. The site was bought by Towles and later extended.

Ironwork by William Dickens of Loughborough in 1946.

The old Power Station in Bridge Street, Loughborough.

This machine, which produced nylon stockings, was the largest ever built by W. Cotton's, *c.*1960.

Some Fine Houses

Contrasting scenes: snow clearing at The Elms, showing the verandah to the drawing room, and a summer's day in the Rock Garden off Leicester Road, Loughborough. The Elms was at one time the residence of Mr E. H. Warner and stood in a fine park of 23 acres, which was for many years the site of flower shows and other big functions. In 1900 Mr A. W. N. Burder bought The Elms after having leased it. He was later to be the owner of the first motor car in the town. By 1950 it had become a Loughborough College Hostel, surrounded on all sides by the new housing of King Edward Road, Albert Promenade, Elms Grove and Lime Avenue.

The handsome and extensive gardens of The Elms. The earliest reference to the house is in John Wood's map of Loughborough, 1837, but the architectural style is that of 1800-1804. The Elms Park Estate was leased to Mr A. W. N. Burder in 1889. He remained there until 1901. The estate was sold off and broken up in 1907. From 1908-1910 it was a nursing home. By the 1950s it was owned by Loughborough College and later by Loughborough University of Technology. The building is still standing (1999).

A gathering of ladies and children outside Field House, Loughborough, *c*.1890s.

Burleigh Fields, Radmoor Road, Loughborough, *c*.1890s. A fine Jacobean house of red brick with stone facings, built *c*.1690. In 1867 it was bought by Dr J. H. Eddowes. Dr Eddowes and his son served Loughborough people as medical practitioners for many years. The lady is probably Mrs Eddowes who lived there until dying in her 86th year, in May 1921. After World War One it was used as a hostel for Loughborough College students. The house had fallen into ruin by 1971 and was demolished in the early 1980s.

Burleigh Hall, Ashby Road, in 1959 when it was the residence of Mr and Mrs Howard Coltman. Built in the early 1700s, it was demolished in 1961.

Mountfields, Forest Road, Loughborough, as it was in the mid-1890s when it was the residence of Joseph Griggs, the first Mayor of Loughborough. He had it built in 1878. It was famous as the venue for his spectacular banquets, fancy dress balls and garden parties.

The Old Rectory, Loughborough. The portion shown here was later demolished.

Afternoon tea in the garden of the Old Rectory in the 1890s, about the time of the Revd Thomas Pitts.

Fairfields, Leicester Road, Loughborough, built in 1823 by the hosiery manufacturer W. White and occupied by his family until 1893. Mrs Augusta Sophia Middleton, wife of the last member of the old Loughborough banking family, lived there until 1922, after which it housed the junior school of the Girls' High School.

A view of The Pines, sometimes known as Holt Cottage but formerly known as either Slee's Farm or Norton's Farm, situated between Forest Road and Holt Drive. The Holt was built for the Griggs family *c.*1820. It was once the home farm of the Holt Estate which was split up to provide land for Glebe House and the Holt University Hostel. It was bought by the County in 1922. In the 1960s the buildings on the left were riding stables. These have since been knocked down. Holt Cottage is still there, only now (1999) it is painted white.

The Lodge, Southfields, at the turn of the century. The lodge was demolished a long time ago, possibly when the estate was purchased by Loughborough Corporation in July 1947.

A group of servants at Southfields Hall, in the late 1890s.

Regent House, Derby Road, Loughborough, the residence of George Hodson Esq when this picture was taken in April 1894.

Two views of the drawing room of Regent House, Derby Road, home of Borough Surveyor George Hodson.

The name of the young lady is not known but the photograph was taken in the garden of Regent House, Derby Road, about 1900.

The Gables, Forest Lane (Forest Road), Loughborough, *c.*1895. At that time it was the home of the Clarke family of local dyeworks fame.

Bell Foundry House. The photograph shows five of the seven children of John William Taylor and Annie Mary Taylor, who died in 1904. This photograph is *c.*1895.

The Beeches, built as Inkerman Cottage *c.*1854 by Loughborough lawyer Alfred Hucknall. In the 1860s it was owned by George Wragg, a linen and woollen draper with premises in the High Street. In the early 1880s, it was acquired by a Mr Jackson who it is thought renamed it The Beeches. It was certainly called that when a Mr Paget moved in about 1887. This photograph was taken in the late 1890s.

Field House on the Ashby Road. It was originally a farmhouse and owned by a Mr Barrow who was a draper in the Market Place in the mid-1840s. Eventually enlarged, in 1933 it passed into the ownership of Loughborough College and was later the residence of Mr G. Board and a boarding house of the College School of which he was headmaster.

Atherstone House in Wards End, built in 1790 by a member of the Atherstone family. Several generations were connected with the local dyeing industry and they owned a bleach yard at the rear of the house and the field across the brook which became part of Queen's Park. In January 1938 the house was demolished to make way for Inland Revenue offices.

The mediaeval Manor House on Sparrow Hill. Sir Edward Hastings, second son of the 1st Earl of Huntingdon lived on the site in 1554, doubtless in this building. In 1999 the building was a restaurant.

The Manor House on Sparrow Hill pictured *c*.1968.

The Grove, one of the fine estates on Ashby Road, Loughborough, erected by William Middleton in 1837. The Middletons were a banking family, their bank being in the Market Place on a site now occupied by the Midland Bank. The Grove was purchased by Loughborough College in 1922 for student accommodation. It was also used as a rehabilitation centre by the RAF during World War Two.

Glebe Farm in Meadow Lane, pictured *c*.1950. It was the last farm to survive in the centre of Loughborough.

Tudor Mansions, formerly known as Woodgate House, was built by Joseph Paget in 1838 and used as a Roman Catholic Rosminian convent for eight years in the 1840s. It was demolished early in 1993, despite the objections of people who cherished its historical significance.

Time Gentleman, Please!

The General Havelock and the Golden Fleece, two pubs at the Fishpool Head, pictured in the 1880s. The roof of the Golden Fleece collapsed on 20 July 1891 and the pub and the adjoining house of the same period were pulled down. In the house was found a curious piece of plasterwork which bore the date 1637, the initials E. M. J. B. and two Prince of Wales' Feathers.

The 'new' Golden Fleece which sprang up on the corner of the Fishpool Head in the 1890s.

The inn on the Loughborough-Quorn road, known by the sign of the Buffalo and Garland. More popularly, however, it was known as the Bull in the Hollow. This photograph was taken in the early 1870s when Joseph Langham was the licensee. Charles Dickens is known to have stayed here overnight.

Two dogs stretch their legs in the Bull's Head Yard, Loughborough.

The Neptune Inn which stood at the High Street end of the Market Place, on a site which later became a shop. When this photograph was taken in 1905, the building was being demolished and the licence transferred to the Empress Ale Stores in Empress Road.

The Three Horse Shoes Inn on Nottingham Road, when Thomas Richards was the landlord. One of the signs in the window offers £10 reward for the return of a lost gold bracelet.

The Mundy Arms, Baxter Gate. A poster on the wall at left advertises a cricket match between Leicestershire and Nottinghamshire to be played at Loughborough.

The Barley Mow, Mill Street (which became Market Street), rebuilt in 1930. The house on the right of the gateway was rebuilt by John Storer at the same time.

The Marquis of Granby stood on the corner of Packhorse Lane and Woodgate. It is photographed some time before its closure in May 1929.

Above: Another photograph of the Marquis of Granby, all boarded up. Now the sign advertising accommodation for cyclists and good stabling has been replaced by one urging the voters of Hastings Ward to vote for Mr Lacey as a councillor and Mr Winterton as the town's Labour MP.

Left: The Red Lion in Biggin Street. Next door is Archie Simpson's family butcher's shop. The pub's licence was removed in 1930 and the following year the premises were bought by the Council for road widening.

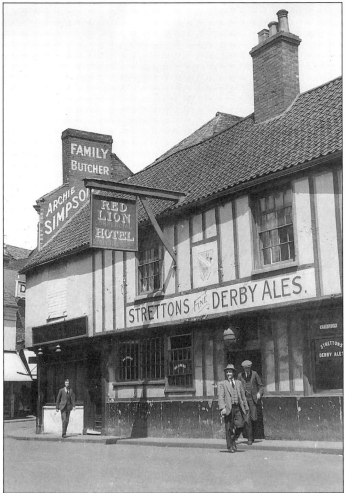

Another photograph of the Red Lion in Biggin Street. By now notices have been posted advertising the pub's fixtures and fittings for sale.

The Blackamoor's Head pub in Loughborough Market Place. It was pulled down and rebuilt in 1933 but has long since vanished altogether.

The Old Bull's Head Hotel in High Street, photographed in 1927 shortly after closing when the licence was transferred to the Bull's Head, Park Road on the Shelthorpe Estate. The sign over the road was removed in February 1928. The inn was first recorded in 1625 but this building dated from 1724 with further enlargements being carried out several times over the next few years.

The Anchor Vaults and the Old Bull's Head Hotel, pictured in the 1920s. A hundred years earlier the Bull's Head had taken over the Anchor Posting House and the sign then advertised the Bull's Head and Anchor.

The Blacksmith's Arms at Wards End, pictured in 1930. The premises were rebuilt in 1931.

Landlord Jack Hewitt, his wife and pub regulars pictured shortly before the Talbot Inn, Market Street, closed down in 1964.

The Lord Nelson pub in the Market Place, pictured in the 1960s. The building later became a Dorothy Perkins shop.

The Old Bell Hotel in the Cattle Market, photographed shortly after it had been sold in 1967.

The Boat Inn, Canal Bank, Meadow Lane, in 1970. Today it looks a great deal smarter.

Transports of Delight

Mrs William Clarke in her carriage outside The Gables, the Clarke residence in Forest Lane. As Laura Wakefield of Hampstead, she had married the youngest son of Thomas Clarke on 9 July 1878.

An outing from the High Street establishment of John Moss in the mid-1890s. Two of his brakes are on the Ashby Road near Gracedieu Priory.

A local hardware dealer and his young helper pose with their horse and wagon in Loughborough between the wars.

A Norton's Dairy cart in 1910.

This horse, pulling a dairy cart, seems very inquisitive and pokes his head into a Loughborough home between the wars.

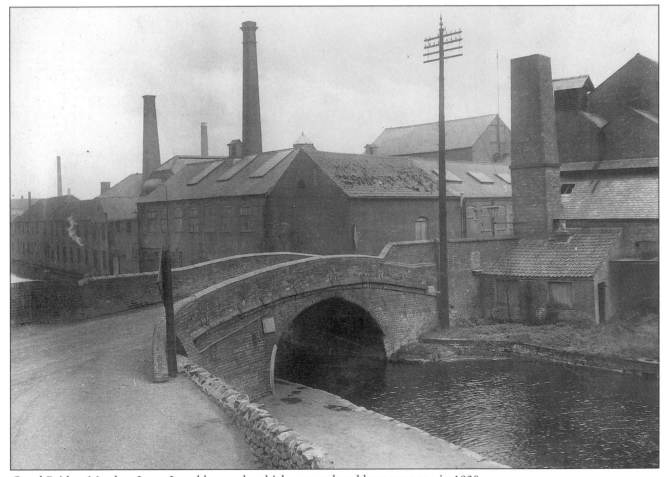

Canal Bridge, Meadow Lane, Loughborough, which was replaced by a new one in 1930.

The Wharf at Loughborough, pictured in 1967.

The canal looking towards Nottingham Road in 1968.

Entering Loughborough Lock in
the late 1960s.

Looking towards Loughborough
Lock from Belton Road Bridge.

A busy summer's day at Loughborough Lock in 1968.

The building of the Manchester, Sheffield & Lincoln Railway (the Great Central) reaches Loughborough in 1895. On the right is Nottingham Road Bridge by the Brush Works. The white fence behind the girls marks the platform on the Midland line. Behind in the centre is the stationmaster's house.

An engine engaged in the construction of the Great Central line at Loughborough in 1895.

Pictured at Loughborough's Derby Road Station in the very late 1890s is a steam coach, together with railway staff.

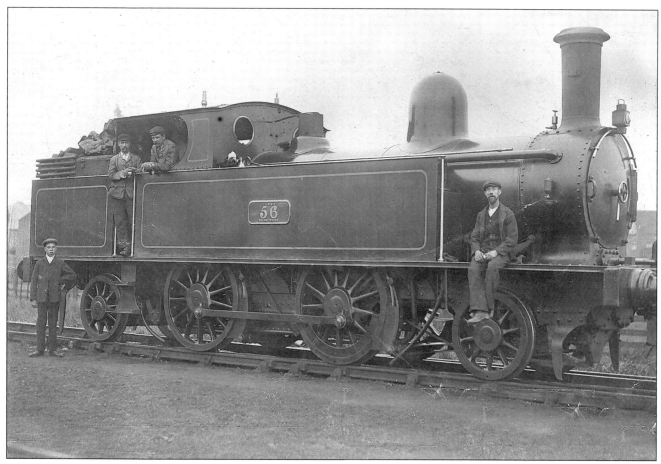

Engine no.56 of the London & North Western Railway Company, pictured at Derby Road Station, which was the terminus of the Charnwood Railway (the 'Bluebell Line'), later the LNWR.

Staff of the Great Central Railway at Loughborough Station in June 1900.

Loughborough's Great Central Station, opened in 1899.

The Derby Road Station in the early part of the 20th century.

Staff at the Great Central Station in 1904.

A foreman and a ticket collector pose with other staff and a horse and carriage at the Midland Station in the 1900s.

The passengers are all aboard at Derby Road Station, waiting for the station staff to have their photograph taken.

Midland Station staff at Loughborough in the 1920s.

Staff outside the Nottingham Road Goods Depot at Loughborough, *c.*1928.

Railway horses and staff at the Midland Station in 1944.

Derby Road Railway Station in 1965.

The former LNER Station at Loughborough in 1968. Originally the Great Central Station, it was to assume that title once more.

This bus ran between Quorn and Shepshed via Loughborough and this picture could be anywhere en route. The bus is a Hallford-Stevens, No D4782, made by W. A. Stevens Ltd, of Maidstone. Built in October 1909, this vehicle was used on hire in Loughborough from September to December 1910 – Loughborough's first motor bus service.

The gentleman in the car in front of The Elms *c.*1900 is either Mr Herbert Morris or Mr Bastert of the world-famous crane manufacturers.

The first White steam car to be seen in Loughborough was the property of Mr W. B. Paget of Southfields Park. Seated in the car are the chauffeur and Mr F. Reynolds, the head gardener, while at the back are Mr Lister (the butler) and Mr T. H. Simpson. The photograph was taken in the early 1900s.

Mr B. C. Hucks and his 70hp Bleriot pictured at Loughborough during the 1912 Daily Mail Aero Circuit.

Loughborough Aerodrome c.1948. It was sited off the Derby Road on what later became the Bishop Meadow Lane Industrial Estate.

Places of Worship

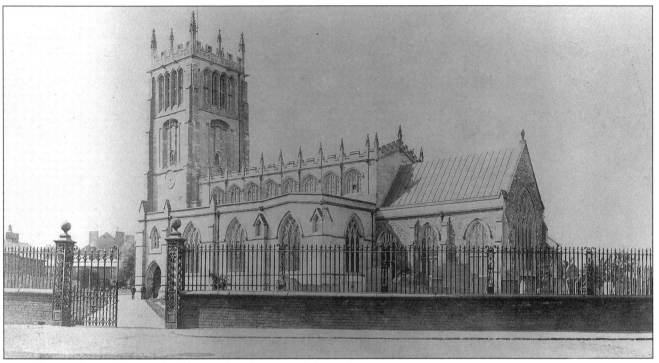

Loughborough Parish Church, All Saints', at the start of the 20th century.

An artist's impression of the chapels at Loughborough Cemetery, Leicester Road. Built in 1857 in Gothic style, it ceased to be used in the 1950s and fell into disrepair. In May 1997 a restoration programme was begun and it is now a Grade II listed building.

Woodgate Baptist Church, now demolished.

Woodgate Sunday School party held at the Catcows Heather farm of Mr Joseph Marsh, *c.*1883.

Woodgate Baptist Church young people's group in the 1890s.

Woodgate Baptist Church choir at Skegness on 20 July 1908.

The United Methodist Free Church in Sparrow Hill as it appeared in the early 1900s. It was erected in 1817.

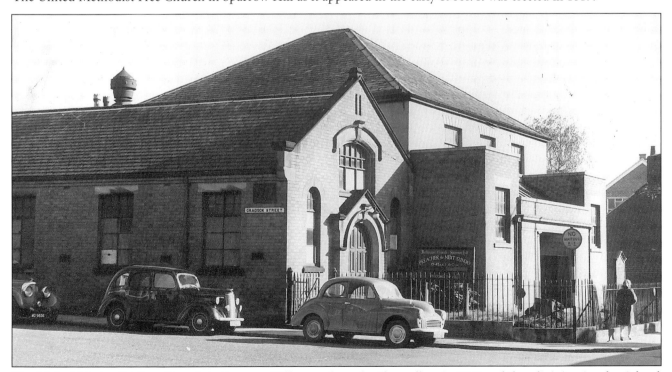

The United Methodist Free Church in Sparrow Hill was enlarged with a gallery in 1828 and the adjoining Sunday School was erected in 1836. The Church was demolished in 1862.

Holy Trinity Church and School before World War One.

Leicestershire Church Lads' Brigade parade at Loughborough on 19 June 1910.

Emmanuel Church, Loughborough, probably pictured between the wars.

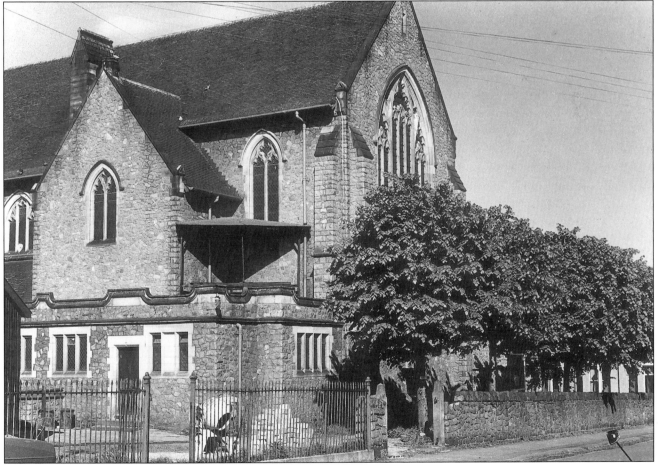

The Parish Church of St Peter's, Loughborough, on Storer Road and the corner of Fearon Street. Built 1910-11 of Mountsorrel Granite (a gift from the Mountsorrel Granite Company). Architects W. S. Weatherley of London and G. H. Barrowcliffe of Loughborough designed and supervised the building of the church.

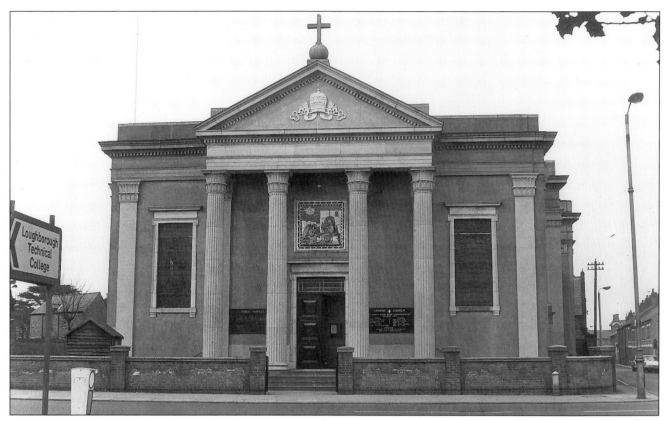

St Mary's Roman Catholic Church on Ashby Road, photographed in 1969.

The Mayor and Town Clerk of Loughborough with church dignatories at St Mary's Roman Catholic Church, probably in the 1930s.

Baxter Gate Baptist Church in 1971.

Loughborough People

Henry Kelsey, headmaster of Cobden Street School, Loughborough, in the 1880s. Alderman Bowler described Kelsey as 'one of the great headmasters of the town'.

Benjamin Baldwin, jeweller of the Market Place, pictured with his four sons. He died on 25 January 1893. It was from his premises that the first experiment in Loughborough of the National Telephone Company was carried out when a line ran between his shop and the King's Head Hotel in High Street.

Councillor George Adock, Mayor of Loughborough 1892-93.

Alderman W. A. Cartwright, Mayor of Loughborough 1893-94 and 1894-95.

Mr and Mrs Marshall Green, photographed at their Bedford Street house in the late 1890s. Marshall Green's gents' outfitters flourishes in the town to this day. In the original building in Baxter Gate they recently celebrated their centenary.

Mrs Hodson and her two sons at Regent House, Derby Road, in April 1894.

An early photograph at Regent House, possibly in the 1880s. The camera stand was one of a number of articles thrown out as unwanted at the sale in January 1958.

Florrie Hodson, elder daughter of George Hodson of Regent House. In 1897 she married Frederick Pare, a Nottingham lace manufacturer.

George Hodson of Regent House was a water engineer and a great personality and stalwart of Loughborough in the closing years of the 19th century and the beginning of the 20th. The building of Blackbrook Reservoir was due mainly to his efforts. He died on 25 April 1907.

Revd S. Wathern Wrigg, one-time vicar of Holy Trinity Church.

Mrs Hole of Shelthorpe House with her children (from left to right) Betty, Peter and Donna.

The six children of Herbert Morris, founder of Herbert Morris Ltd.

Christabel and Maclean Burder on the verandah of The Elms.

For years, generations of Eddowes were doctors in the Market Place and lived over their surgery in the fine old house which later became the Maypole Dairy. Here is the last of the Eddowes to practise medicine in the Market Place.

Mr C. Duffner came to Loughborough from the Black Forest area of Germany in about 1870. He took over King's jeweller's business in the Market Place six years later and about 1889 rebuilt the premises in Bavarian style. On holiday in Germany when World War One broke out, he and his daughter were forced to remain there until peace was declared. He returned to England and died on 21 December 1937, aged 97.

The identity of this group is not known but they were probably a group of amateur actors.

Gypsy life outside Loughborough, *c.*1910.

'Lemmy' Holmes was one of Loughborough's best-known characters at the turn of the century.

John Higgs of 8 Havelock Street, Loughborough with his wife. He was locomotive driver and foreman on the Charnwood Forest Railway branch of the LNWR from 1908 to 1929.

Charles Moss, William Cartwright, Thomas Mayo and Tom Towle on holiday at Oran before World War One.

The Lowes of Limehurst House, Loughborough. Mr and Mrs Lowe are pictured with their ten children, all of whom still lived at home. It was the eve of World War One, however, and on the morning that Ernest Albert, the eldest son, left to join the Army, the family assembled outside before breakfast to have their photograph taken.

The Mayor of Loughborough, Alderman G. H. Bowler JP, judging a beautiful baby competition in the 1920s.

Councillor Alan Moss, Mayor of Loughborough 1927-28 and 1928-29.

Coalman Dan Huntington of Burton-on-the-Wolds retired in 1947 after 45 years service. This photograph was taken in Loughborough.

Carilloneurs Sidney Potter (left) and Eric Jordan, pictured in 1932.

Hilda Dormer was the first Lady Mayor of Loughborough (1947-48) and died in office. This photograph is from the collection of Catherine Brooks.

The Mayor of Loughborough, Nancy Cope, and her daughter, Jean, at an international supper at the YMCA on Great Central Road in 1955.

Events & Celebrations

Unveiling the Fearon Fountain in Loughborough Market Place in 1870. The fountain was paid for by Archdeacon Henry Fearon of All Saints' Church, who had led a hard-fought but successful campaign for the town to be supplied with fresh water at a time when water-borne diseases such as cholera and typhoid were rife.

The first meet of the Quorn Hounds in Loughborough Market Place on Easter Tuesday, 1894. In accepting the invitation, Lord Lonsdale wrote that they had previously avoided the town because of the noise of spectators alarming the pack. 'In view of this it is to be hoped that all who witness the Meet next Tuesday will endeavour to preserve order,' said one local newspaper.

Loughborough Pleasure Fair *c*.1894.

Loughborough Market Place is decked out for the golden jubilee celebrations for Queen Victoria in June 1887.

Ten years later and the Market Place is again awash with people, bunting and flags, this time for Queen Victoria's diamond jubilee.

The Charnwood Forest Railway Hotel management have made a particularly fine effort to decorate the establishment for Queen Victoria's diamond jubilee.

A gentleman dismounts from his bicycle and ladies in their finery, together with a small boy pose for the camera outside a Loughborough building decorated for Queen Victoria's diamond jubilee.

Helpers pose inside a refreshment marquee at the Hospital Bazaar held at Southfields Park, June 1895.

The exterior and interior of the Bon Bon Stall at the Hospital Bazaar held at Southfields Park in June 1895.

Small children await their turn on the carousel at Lougborough's November Fair, *c.*1890s.

Loughborough Primitive Methodists lead the parade in the Market Place as the town marks the coronation of King Edward VII in 1902.

Boys gather round the decorations in Loughborough Market Place for the coronation of King Edward VII. The first building on the left, that of Armstrong's general furniture warehouse, was later leased to F. W. Woolworth. Next to it is the Midland Counties General Bank.

Granby Street is bedecked for Edward VII's coronation.

High Street in 1902, decorated for the coronation of King Edward VII.

Crowds gather outside Loughborough's Parish Church during the funeral service, in London, of Edward VII in 1910.

The proclamation of King George V in the Market Place on 9 May 1910. The Mayor, Alderman Thomas Mayo, leads the cheering.

Crowds in front of Loughborough Town Hall on 22 June 1911, on the occasion of King George V's coronation. The gentleman in the top hat is John Moss, the former High Street butcher.

Loughborough townsfolk, dressed in their best clothes, mingle in the Cattle Market in June 1911 to celebrate George V's coronation.

The parade continues along Granby Street in June 1911 as Loughborough marks King George V's coronation.

A civic procession, part of the town's celebrations for the coronation of King George V, passes the Free Library in Granby Street on 22 June 1911.

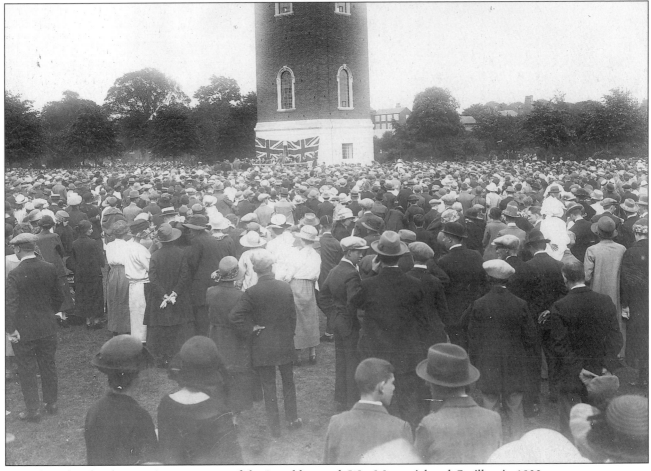

Crowds gather for the opening ceremony of the Loughborough War Memorial and Carillon in 1923.

Dignitaries leaving Queen's Park after the opening of the War Memorial and Carillon.

Guests at the Loughborough Lady Clerks' Leap Year Ball in 1928.

Mayoral procession to mark the installation of Councillor John Shadlock Marr, who was Mayor of Loughborough twice, in 1933-34 and 1934-35. Councillor Marr ran a clothing shop in Church Gate and was also a pawnbroker.

The Quorn Hunt meets in Loughborough Market Place.

Crowds in the Market Place for the silver jubilee celebrations of King George V in 1935.

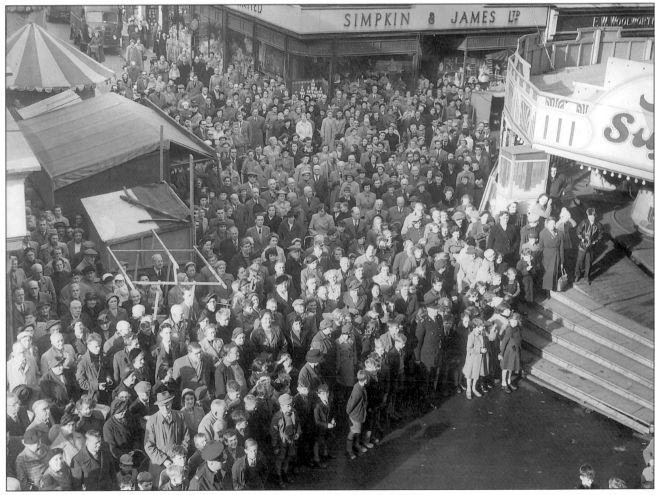

Loughborough people gather for the 1955 November Fair in the Market Place.

Loughborough at War

Horses and riders of the Loughborough Yeomanry off to camp on 22 May 1914. They are riding through Bridge Street, later the site of the fire station which was built in 1930.

Men who have just enlisted in the Leicestershire Regiment, pictured at Loughborough Railway Station in 1914.

The 5th Battalion, Leicestershire Regiment, parading in Loughborough on 11 August 1914.

Loughborough Market Place is the scene of a parade of soldiers from the Leicestershire Regiment during World War One.

Children of Loughborough men serving in World War One are entertained at the Picture House on Ashby Road in December 1914. The shops on the right were later demolished for the erection of part of the College.

A small crowd inspects bomb damage in the Rushes after a Zeppelin raid on Loughborough on 31 January 1916. Four men and six women were killed, five men and seven women injured. The Blue Boar Inn is next to the Rising Sun Lodging House. The Electric Station chimney can be seen in the background.

Premises at the rear of the Crown and Cushion Inn,
Loughborough, after the air-raid of 31 January 1916.

Bomb damage on Empress Road, Loughborough,
after the 1916 raid.

Mrs Arthur Armstrong, Mrs Walter Coltman, Miss Coltman and Miss F. H. Cayless pictured at a stall at the Town Hall on Alexandra Day in 1917.

Alexandra Day collectors outside the Town Hall in 1918.

Wounded soldiers, and some of those who nursed them, pictured at Loughborough Hospital in June 1917.

Peace was restored in 1918 and the following year members of the Leicestershire Regiment paraded in Loughborough Market Place once more as thousands turned out to greet them.

'We're having a good time somewhere in Loughborough,' says the original caption on this photograph of members of the Leicestershire Regiment taken on 26 October 1939, nearly two months after the outbreak of World War Two.

Loughborough air-raid wardens line up to meet the Duchess of Gloucester on 13 August 1940.

Loughborough members of the Auxiliary Fire Service wait to meet the Duchess of Gloucester in August 1940.

A mobile first-aid unit on parade awaiting for the Duchess of Gloucester at Loughborough in August 1940.

Personnel of the St John Ambulance Brigade taking part in a combined services parade at Loughborough on 15 April 1941.

The Mayor of Loughborough, Councillor G. H. Dean, and the Mayoress, pictured with Leicestershire men who had returned from Norway in May 1940.

Soldiers of the Leicestershire Regiment, almost certainly including Loughborough men, give a cheery thumbs-up outside Leicester's London Road Station in May 1940 after their return from Norway.

The scene at Loughborough Labour Exchange in January 1941, when the '36' class as well as 20-year-olds registered under the National Defence (Armed Forces) Acts. There was only one conscientious objector out of 224 registered.

Loughborough's first surface street air-raid shelters being built in Ratcliffe Road in February 1941.

Four months later, in June 1941, and surface shelters are completed. They were erected in congested areas, ran the whole length of streets and had small spaces between them for 'pig bins', where kitchen scraps were collected for use on the Corporation pig farm.

A Luftwaffe aerial photograph map of Loughborough dated 1941, with the Brush Works highlighted.

Evacuee children and their mothers sit down to tea at a Christmas party held at the Brush Sports Club in Fennel Street in 1941.

Air-raid wardens pictured in front of Loughborough Town Hall in December 1941.

Mr George Mitchell (centre, with the stirrup pump) was the organiser of this Curzon Street, Loughborough, firewatching party in January 1941.

Mr Howard Coltman, standing second left behind the ploughing machine, was one of the organisers of a Farmers' Day during Loughborough's War Weapons Week in February 1942. He lived at Burleigh Hall, off Ashby Road, and was later awarded an OBE and an honorary MA.

A youth parade in Loughborough Market Place as part of the War Weapons Week in February 1942.

Loughborough townsfolk watching a demonstration of fire-fighting during the Second World War.

Members of a Loughborough Home Guard unit pictured in 1942.

Herbert Schofield, principal of Loughborough College (seated centre) pictured with other staff and locally-based servicemen. This group includes troops of the US 82nd Airborne Division based at Quorn in 1944. A few weeks later, the Americans left to take part in the D-Day landings in Normandy.

With the war almost won and the threat of invasion over, the Home Guard was disbanded. This group photograph is of the 9th (Loughborough) Battalion under the command of Lieutenant-Colonel S. K. Lewis (third from the right, front row).

Fire and Police

Members of the Loughborough Police Division in 1886.

The Loughborough Borough Police Force *c*.1905.

The Loughborough Division of the Leicestershire Special Constabulary in 1940.

Loughborough Fire Brigade, photographed in front of the old Free Library in 1887. Standing (left to right) are Jabez Cliff (foreman), A. Preston, W. Hammonds, George Clements (superintendent), Hopkins, R. Marriott and R. Poole. On the engine are T. Hudson (driver), W. Wesley (foreman), Kirk, Fletcher, D. Gilbert (turncock) and A. Lockwood (engineer).

Loughborough Fire Brigade exercise in Granby Street, their engine is still horse-drawn.

Four members of Loughborough Fire Brigade pose before a steam-driven fire engine.

Loughborough Fire Brigade men with their new engine behind the old Town Offices in Ashby Road in 1899.

Fighting a fire somewhere in Loughborough early in the 20th century. The fire brigade do not appear to have arrived and local men train a hose upon the burning building.

Firemen pose proudly with two engines in Loughborough, *c*.1925.

Societies and Organisations

Loughborough allotment holders at their annual vegetable show, *c.*1890s. They are pictured on the bowling green of the Station Hotel on Derby Road. The tall bearded man (back row, sixth from the left) was a member of the Leicestershire Constabulary.

A group called the Loughborough Ringers, pictured c.1895. It is thought they were handbell ringers.

The Girls' Club in Biggin Street, forerunner of the YWCA. The premises were taken over by Harry Rayson, furnisher, in January 1926.

A group of men photographed outside the old YMCA building in Granby Street in the early 1930s.

Founders of the Beacon Lodge of Freemasons in Loughborough.

Members of the Loyal Sovereign Lodge of Manchester Unity Oddfellows Society in Loughborough, marking the restoration of the Oddfellows Hall in the town in October 1931. It was originally built as a theatre in 1822 and the artists came up steps from below ground to reach the stage. The theatre was not a success and the Oddfellows purchased it in 1856, after it had been closed for a few years. They themselves disposed of it in 1945, when it became an auctioneers' mart, Adkinson & Freckelton, and it later became a cycle shop, then Cunnington's carpet shop. The building, in Sparrow Hill, is still standing.

Members of the Loughborough and District Employment Committee, photographed in September 1960 to mark the golden jubilee of the Employment Service Exchange.

Schools and Colleges

These little boys and girls were members of Class 5 at St Mary's Roman Catholic School, Loughborough, c.1895.

A group of Board School pupils, c.1900.

Another Loughborough Board School group from around the turn of the century.

Class from Church Gate Infants' School in 1910.

Church Gate School in the late 1890s.

Church Gate Schoolboys enjoy an outing to Breedon and Tonge (near Melbourne) in the 1930s.

Inscriptions over the doorway of Burton Church Gate Schools.

Loughborough Grammar School staff and pupils photographed from the Quad, *c.*1890s.

Loughborough Grammar School, in the 1920s or 1930s.

The Union flag flutters over Loughborough Grammar School in 1952 and loyal greetings are displayed to the new queen.

Teaching staff of the Girls' High School, Loughborough, in 1906. Seated (left to right) are Miss Davies, Miss Rose (art), Miss Peters (science) and Miss Grimley.

The Natural Science Room at Loughborough High School for Girls, c.1906.

The main corridor of Loughborough High School for Girls, c.1906 when Miss Mary Walmsley MA was headmistress. She had gained a Natural Science Tripos Honours Degree from Cambridge University.

Loughborough High School for Girls, *c.*1906, pictured from the school garden.

The dining hall at Loughborough High School for Girls, *c.*1906.

Loughborough Technical College staff in 1918, pictured in front of the Instructional Factory.

Loughborough Technical College teaching staff of 1920.

Members of the Loughborough College Cadet Corps photographed on 9 November 1939, two months after the outbreak of World War Two.

Loughborough Colleges Union Council of 1957-58. Back row (left to right): P. Gilbert, J. M. Green, J. J. Freeman, V. K. Bahree (entrance secretary), R. D. Willmott, D. J. Leeding, T. E. Scott, J. N. Hardwick, E. J. Shurvinton. Front row: D. A. Heeley (internal affairs), D. J. Arterton (students' secretary), M. G. Beck (LEA vice-president), F. Island (president), J. Giles (engineering vice-president), C. D. Shargool (students' treasurer) and D. M. Chibututu (external affairs).

Sporting Affairs

The Southfields Hall cricket team in the late 1890s.

Loughborough Town Cricket Club at their Park Road ground before World War One.

Loughborough Parish Church Cricket Club, 1896.

Loughborough Trinity FC, 1898-99. They were members of the Leicestershire FA and the Loughborough and District Junior League.

Loughborough Corinthians FC, 1898-99. They were champions of the Loughborough and District League Division Two.

Loughborough Corinthians FC, 1902-03, winners of the Loughborough Charity Cup.

Loughborough Casual FC, 1899-1900, members of the Loughborough and District League.

Loughborough Victoria Rovers FC, season 1901-02.

Loughborough Amateurs FC, season 1902-03.

Loughborough Mutuals FC, 1904-05. They were runners-up in the Loughborough and District League and reached the semi-finals of the Leicestershire County Shield.

W. Atkin's team which met Loughborough Wednesday FC on 17 December 1913.

Loughborough Old Boys FC, season 1913-14.

Loughborough College FC in the 1920s. The college principal, Herbert Schofield, is pictured seated extreme right.

The successful Brush Works FC team pictured with their trophies in 1936-37.

Loughborough College rugby union team in 1921. College principal Herbert Schofield is seated fourth from the left, wearing spats.

Famous Loughborough athlete George Brewill pictured with some of his many trophies. He started his athletics career at the age of ten, at Newark, and became renowned as the finest sprinter in Leicestershire. He was also a founder member of Loughborough Corinthians FC and after playing right-back for them he became chairman of the management committee for many years. He was the first manager of the Westminster Bank's Shepshed branch and later took over the Nottingham and Nottinghamshire Bank (later the Westminster Bank) in the Cattle Market, Loughborough. He retired in 1940 and died on 22 April 1958, aged 74.

A group of Loughborough bowls enthusiasts. No date is given for the picture but it is known that John Randall (extreme left of the front row) was killed while riding his bicycle on Ashby Road on 31 January 1912.

Loughborough's Station Hotel Bowling Club members, winners of the Fred Armstrong Charity Cup in 1917.

The 1918 Fred Armstrong Charity Cup winners, Queen's Park Bowling Club.

Queen's Park Bowling Club members pictured in 1928. The club is still going strong in Loughborough.

A pleasant afternoon in the 1890s on the Swan Boats at Burleigh Brook Park on Ashby Road. It was popularly known as 'Ticklebelly Park', to the vexation of the owner, who sought to maintain a high moral tone.

An outing of the Loughborough Boat Club to Red Hill in the 1890s.

A group photographed at The Willows on Derby Road on a Sunday afternoon in 1909. The trophies are for rowing in the junior fours in the Loughborough Boat Club regatta.

Members of Loughborough Boat Club at the club's annual regatta some time before World War One.

Loughborough Boat Club members pictured in 1932.

Rural Reflections

A wonderful rural scene at Dishley Mill at the turn of the century.

Another view of Dishley Mill.

Flooding on the Derby Road at Dishley in August 1912.

Shelthorpe Cottage, which later became The Cedars, off Leicester Road, almost opposite the cemetery. A date of 1797 appeared on the wall but the major portion was erected in 1826 by a wine merchant called Mott. When a Mr Ward occupied it in the 1840s he called it Searlesthorpe Cottage. In 1895 it was purchased by the Great Central Railway. This picture is dated c.1904 when Mr Walter Coltman occupied the house.

Shelthorpe Hall, near Loughborough. Built *c.*1850, possibly by the Hole family which was connected with the house on and off throughout its life. They were occupying it at the time of its demolition (1959). Rented by John William Taylor of the Bell Foundry in 1859, he sub-let it occasionally. In 1887 C. W. C. Middleton JP, the banker, was living there. In 1889 the tenant was W. F. Beardsley, the solicitor. In May 1889 the house was purchased by John William Taylor for £4,000. This photograph was taken *c.*1898 when owned by the Taylor family.

The Bull's Head, Shelthorpe, *c.*1929. This is now a McDonalds!

Shelthorpe Estate, newly-built in *c.*1946. Loughborough Town Council started building Shelthorpe Estate in 1927 and had reached as far as Griggs Road by the outbreak of war in 1939. Development then ceased, to be resumed after hostilities had ended. By November 1946 there were 47 new houses built.

Garendon Hall, erected by Samuel Phillipps in the middle of the 18th century. The Mansard roof was added at the end of the 19th century.

The Triumphal Arch at Garendon Hall, erected *c.*1730.

Seated by the door of Garendon Hall, c.1908, is Everard March Phillipps De Lisle.

The gardener's cottage at Garendon Hall.

Ornamental gardens and 'cottage' at Garendon, demolished *c.*1943.

The De Lisle homecoming. On 26 June 1907, the De Lisles returned to Garendon Hall. They had been living in comparative retirement since 1883 while their estates recovered from the crippling blow dealt them by Everard De Lisle's grandfather who had spent the income of three generations instead of that of one life tenant. During the absence of the De Lisles, the mansion had been let to the Marquis de Salicito and to Mr Lucas Tooth.

The servants of Garendon Hall, *c.*1890s.

Cotes, near Loughborough. The village is still quite separate from Loughborough, as it was in the days when these ladies could stop for an unhurried chat. But the planners have lately been proposing a big house-building programme.

Another view of Cotes. The thatched cottages are suggestive of rural torpor, but Cotes once had a mansion house which entertained royalty. In 1603 the Queen of James I and her son, Prince Henry, spent the night at 'Cotes Castle' and later Charles I paid a visit en route to the siege of Leicester. The castle was eventually destroyed by an accidental fire in 1645.

Cotes Mill, near Loughborough. Two mills were mentioned in the Domesday Book of 1085. They belonged to the manor and all Loughborough people were obliged to take their corn to be ground there. It is now a popular restaurant.

Cotes Bridge, pictured in 1968.

Boys of the 1st Nanpantan
Scouts at camp in 1911.

Staff of the Longcliffe Hotel at
Nanpantan on 25 June 1899.

Below: Holywell Haw,
Nanpantan, birthplace of John
Chapman, the clockmaker, in
1754. (Haw was the name given
to an enclosure of land effected
by means of a hawthorn hedge.)
The house, which survives today
as a farmhouse, is associated with
a fairy-tale legend.

The Priory Hotel, Nanpantan, *c.*1960s.

A garden fete at Nanpantan Hall in 1926.

A picnic at Blackbrook Reservoir, June 1906.

The first of these three photographs shows Thorpe Village in 1902; the other two photographs of the village were taken in 1931.

Looking from from Thorpe Hill towards Derby Road (now the Alan Moss Estate) in 1946.

Thorpe Hill and village in 1947.

This group of old thatched cottages at Thorpe Acre made a very rural picture in the early years of the 20th century.

Thorpe Acre Vicarage as it stood in the early 1900s, this photograph probably having been taken in the summer of 1905.

Swift's Cottage at Thorpe Acre in 1967.

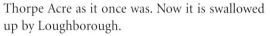

Thorpe Acre as it once was. Now it is swallowed up by Loughborough.

Thorpe Acre Village in 1966.

The Plough Inn at Thorpe Acre in 1970.

The old Knightthorpe Hall, Knightthorpe, another area which is now part of Loughborough.